Edmund Rogers

Beauty and the Beast

a humorous cantata for solo voices - S.C.T.B. - chorus & orchestra

Edmund Rogers

Beauty and the Beast
a humorous cantata for solo voices - S.C.T.B. - chorus & orchestra

ISBN/EAN: 9783337349677

Printed in Europe, USA, Canada, Australia, Japan

Cover: Foto ©Thomas Meinert / pixelio.de

More available books at **www.hansebooks.com**

Beauty and the Beast.

A HUMOROUS CANTATA

FOR SOLO VOICES (S.C.T.B.) CHORUS & ORCHESTRA.

Words by kind permission from

"DEAN'S PANTOMIME TOY TALE BOOK."

Music by

Edmund Rogers,

Composer of "JACK AND THE BEANSTALK"," BLUE BEARD", &c.

Ent : Sta : Hall.   *Price 3/= nett.*

LONDON:
WEEKES & Cº,
14. Hanover Street, Regent Street, W.

THE FULL SCORE AND ORCHESTRAL PARTS MAY BE HIRED FROM THE PUBLISHERS.

CONTENTS.

BEAUTY AND THE BEAST.

OVERTURE.

EDMUND ROGERS.

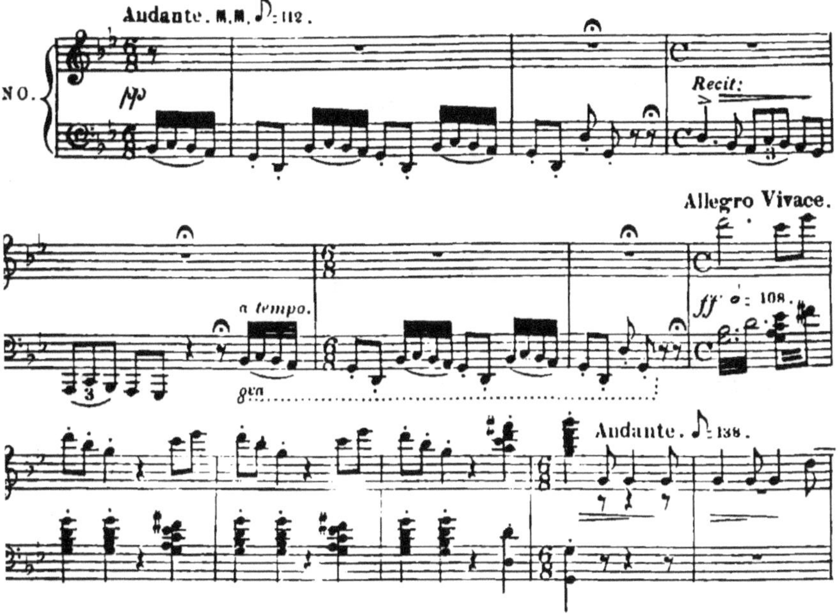

Allegretto. ♩ = 88.

leggiero.

f
f
Ped.
affettuoso.
p
Ped.
Ped.
Ped.
C
Recit:
3
3
Allegro Vivace. 𝅗𝅥= 108.
ff

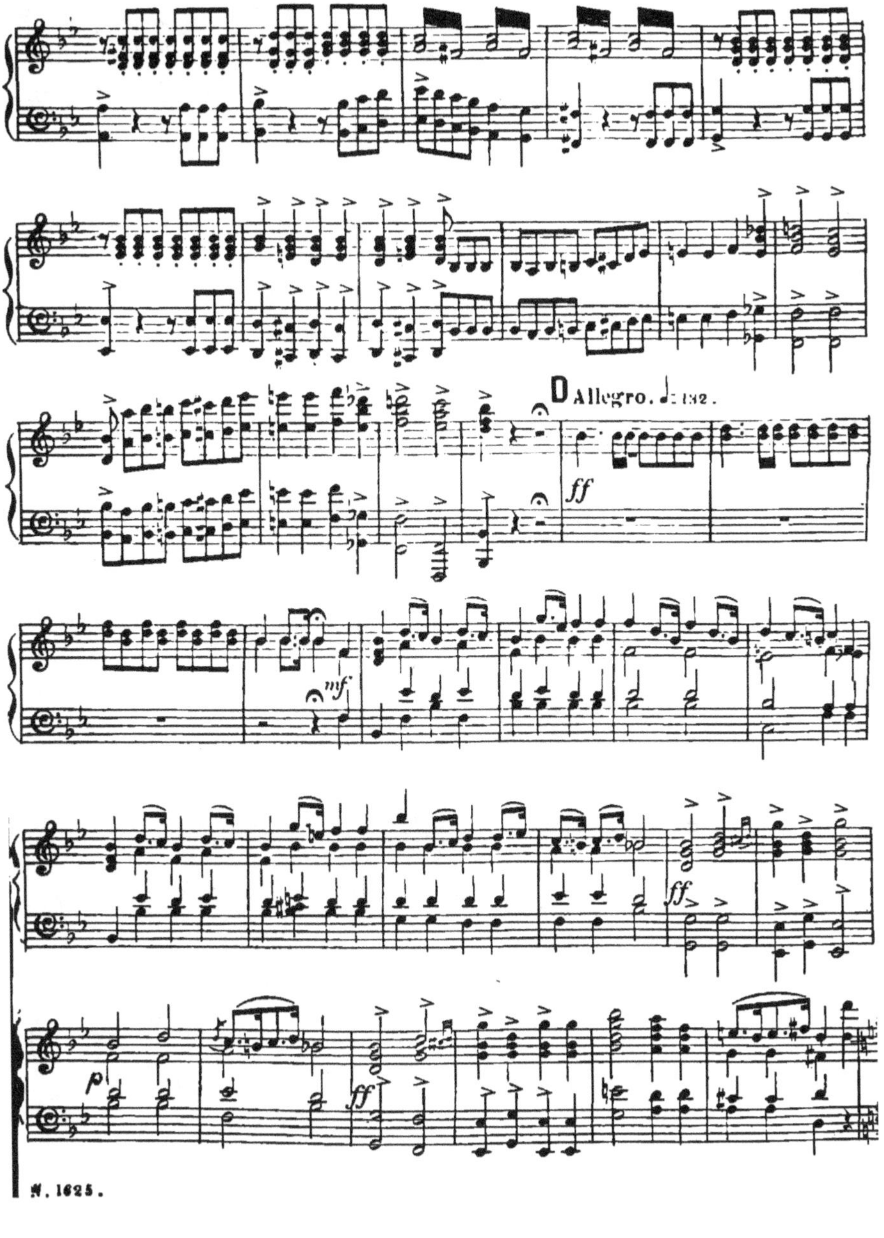
D Allegro. ♩= 132.
ff
mf
ff
p
ff

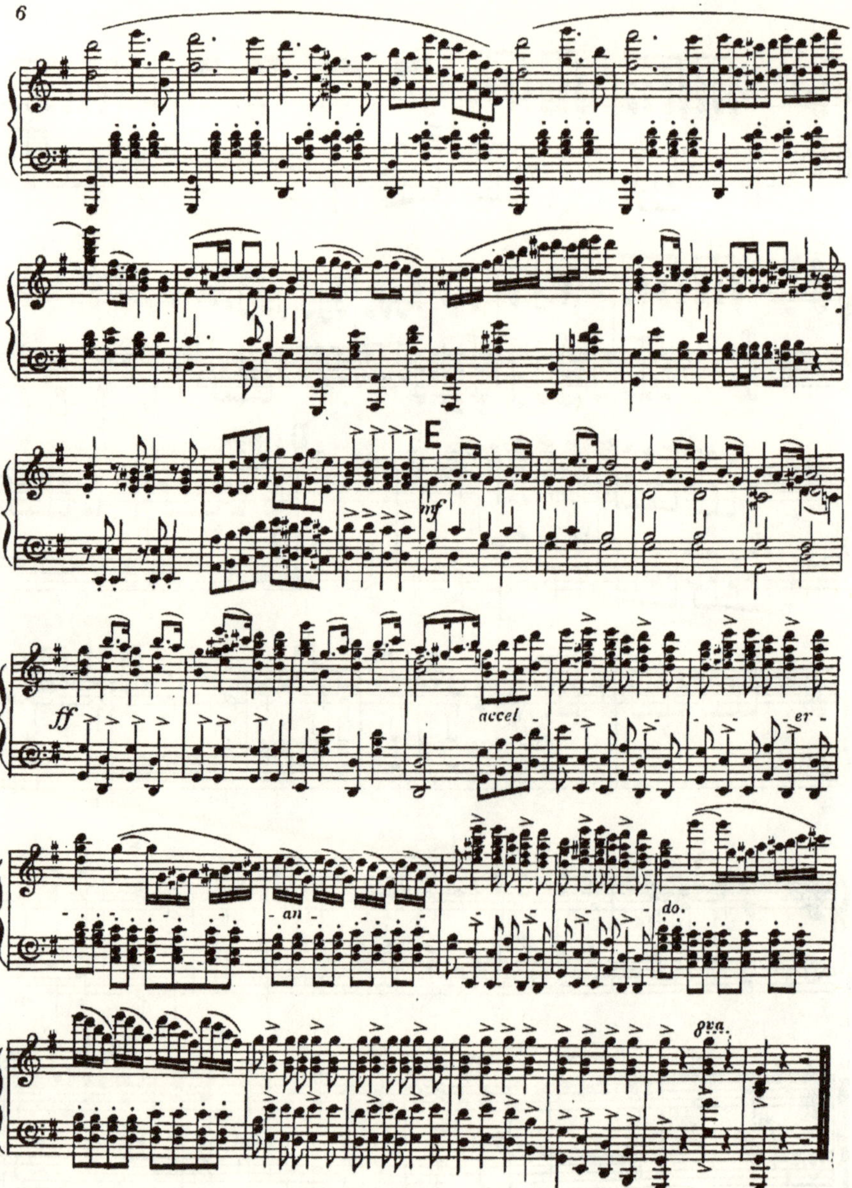
E
mf
ff
accel
er
an
do.
8va

No 1.

M. ♩ = 108.

Allegro
Moderato.

SOPRANO.

CONTRALTO. A Mer-chant, who liv'd long a-go in the East, Was

TENOR. A Mer-chant, who liv'd long a-go in the East,

BASS. A Mer-chant, who liv'd long a-go in the East, Was

A Mer-chant, who liv'd long a-go in the East,

bless'd with three daugh-ters, We're told so at least,— But the two which were el-der, we

We're told so at least,— But the two which were el-der, we

bless'd with three daugh-ters, We're told so at least,— But the two which were el-der, we

We're told so at least,— But the two which were el-der, we

can_ - not re_frain From frank_ly des_crib_ing as cer_tain_ly 'plain,' From
can_ - not re_frain From frank_ly des_crib_ing as cer_tain_ly 'plain,' From
can_ - not re_frain From frank_ly des_crib_ing as cer_tain_ly 'plain,' From
can_not re_frain From frank_ly des_crib_ing as cer_tain_ly 'plain,' From
frank_ly des_crib_ing as cer_tain_ly, cer_tain_ly 'plain;' A
frank_ly des_crib_ing as cer_tain_ly, cer_tain_ly 'plain;' A
frank_ly des_crib_ing as cer_tain_ly, cer_tain_ly 'plain;' A
frank_ly des_crib_ing as cer_tain_ly, cer_tain_ly 'plain;' A
A
Mer_chant, who liv'd long a_ - go in the East, Was bless'd with three daugh_ters, We're
Mer_chant, who liv'd long a_ - go in the East, We're
Mer_chant, who liv'd long a_ - go in the East, Was bless'd with three daugh_ters, We're
Mer_chant, who liv'd long a_ - go in the East, We're

t least,— But the two that were el_der, we can_not re_frain From

t least,— But the two that were el_der, we can_not re_frain From

t least,— But the two that were el_der, we can_not re_frain From

t least,— But the two that were el_der, we can_not re_frain From

ng as cer_tain_ly'plain;' But the two that were el_der, we can_not re_frain From

ng as cer_tain_ly'plain;' But the two that were el_der, we can_not re_frain From

ng as cer_tain_ly'plain;' But the two that were el_der, we can_not re_frain From

g as cer_tain_ly'plain;' But the two that were el_der, we can_not re_frain From

B

as cer_tain_ly, cer_tain_ly 'plain;'

as cer_tain_ly, cer_tain_ly 'plain;'

as cer_tain_ly, cer_tain_ly 'plain;' And as they were want_ing in

as cer_tain_ly, cer_tain_ly 'plain;'

10

charms of the face, *mf* For, as

They made up for bad looks with much rib-bon and lace; For, as

Must al-ways have some-thing be-com-ing to wear, Must

Must al-ways have some-thing be-com-ing to wear, Must

na-ture was want-ing, the trou-ble-some pair Must al-ways have some-thing be-com-ing to wear, Must

na-ture was want-ing, the trou-ble-some pair Must al-ways have some-thing be-com-ing to wear, Must

C

al-ways have some-thing be-com-ing to wear.

al-ways have some-thing be-com-ing to wear.

al-ways have some-thing be-com-ing to wear. *f*

They were

al-ways have some-thing be-com-ing to wear. Then of course they were jea-lous, their man-ners were sour;

And, in
And, in
ne - ver good - tem - per'd for more than an hour, And, in
And, in
D
fact, they could ne - ver re - mem - ber their du - ty To a
fact, they could ne - ver re - mem - ber their du - ty To a
fact, they could ne - ver re - mem - ber their du - ty To a
fact, they could ne - ver re - mem - ber their du - ty To a
rall.
a tempo.
sis - ter so fair that the folks call'd her Beau - ty. A
sis - ter so fair that the folks call'd her Beau - ty. A
sis - ter so fair that the folks call'd her Beau - ty. A
sis - ter so fair that the folks call'd her Beau - ty. A

Mer _ chant, who liv'd... long a _ go in the East,

Mer _ chant, who liv'd... long a _ go in the East,

Mer _ chant, who liv'd... long a _ go in the East, Was

Mer _ chant, who liv'd... long a _ go in the East,

We're told so, at least;___ But the

We're told so, at least;___ But the

bless'd with three daugh _ ters, We're told so, at least;___ But the

We're told so, at least;___ But the

two which were el _ der, we can _ not re _ frain From

two which were el _ der, we can _ not re _ frain From

two which were el _ der, we can _ not re _ frain From

two which were el _ der, we can _ not re _ frain From

frank_ly des_crib_ing as cer_tain_ly 'plain;' From frank_ly des_crib_ing as cer_tain_ly, cer_tain_ly

frank_ly des_crib_ing as cer_tain_ly 'plain;' From frank_ly des_crib_ing as cer_tain_ly, cer_tain_ly

frank_ly des_crib_ing as cer_tain_ly 'plain:' From frank_ly des_crib_ing as cer_tain_ly, cer_tain_ly

frank_ly des_crib_ing as cer_tain_ly 'plain;' From frank_ly des_crib_ing as cer_tain_ly, cer_tain_ly

'plain;' Then of course they were jea _ lous, Their

'plain;' Then of course they were jea _ lous, Their

'plain;' Then of course they were jea _ lous, Their

'plain;' Then of course they were jea _ lous, Their

man _ ners were sour; for more than an hour,__ And, in

man _ ners were sour; for more than an hour,__ And, in

man _ ners were sour; They were ne _ ver good_tem_per'd for more than an hour,__ And, in

man _ ners were sour; for more than an hour,__ And, in

fact, they could ne _ ver re _ mem _ ber their du _ ty To a

fact, they could ne _ ver re _ mem _ ber their du _ ty To a

fact, they could ne _ ver re _ mem _ ber their du _ ty To a

fact, they could ne _ ver re _ mem _ ber their du _ ty To a

E

sis _ ter so fair that the folks call'd her *Beau _ ty*, And, in

sis _ ter so fair that the folks call'd her *Beau _ ty*, And, in

sis _ ter so fair that the folks call'd her *Beau _ ty*, And, in

sis _ ter so fair that the folks call'd her *Beau _ ty*, And, in

fact, they could ne _ ver re _ mem _ ber their du _ ty To a

fact, they could ne _ ver re _ mem _ ber their du _ ty To a

fact, they could ne _ ver re _ mem _ ber their du _ ty To a

fact, they could ne _ ver re _ mem _ ber their du _ ty To a

sis-ter so fair that the folks call'd... her Beau-ty. And, in

sis-ter so fair that the folks call'd... her Beau-ty. And, in

sis-ter so fair that the folks call'd... her Beau-ty. And, in

sis-ter so fair that the folks call'd... her Beau-ty. And, in

ff rall: e

stentate.

fact, they could ne-ver re-mem-ber their du-ty To a sis-ter so fair that the

fact, they could ne-ver re-mem-ber their du-ty To a sis-ter so fair that the

fact, they could ne-ver re-mem-ber their du-ty To a sis-ter so fair that the

fact, they could ne-ver re-mem-ber their du-ty To a sis-ter so fair that the

folks call'd her *Beauty.*

folks call'd her *Beauty.*

folks call'd her *Beauty.*

folks call'd her *Beauty.*

a tempo

ARIA.—"NOW A GREAT ENCHANTER THEREABOUTS." & CHORUS.

N.º 2.

(CONTRALTO.)

Andantino. M.M. ♪ = 188.

VOICE.

PIANO.

Now a great En chan ter

there a bouts Could work a po tent charm, To do to ev' ry

bo dy else All sorts of grievous harm, All sorts of griev ous harm. His

on ly plea sure was to hurt, And that he thought de light ful; In

W. 1625.

fact the En_chan_ter on_ly liv'd For sake of be_ing spiteful, spiteful,
f
spite_ful.
A
And so be chang'd a hand_some Prince, (And
p
CHORUS.
f
A wick_ed thing to do! . . .
none so fine be_fore or since,) A wick_ed thing to do! . . .
SOLO.
In_to the like_ness
A wick_ed thing to do! . . .
A wick_ed thing to do! . . .
of. . . a bear, Such as. . . they see who like to spare A six_pence for the

CHORUS.

A six-pence for the 'Zoo!'... A

'Zoo!' A six-pence for the 'Zoo!'... A six-pence for the 'Zoo!' 'Zoo!' 'Zoo!' A

A six-pence for the 'Zoo!' 'Zoo!' 'Zoo!' A

A six-pence for the 'Zoo!' 'Zoo!' 'Zoo!' A-

B

six - pence for the 'Zoo!'

six - pence for the 'Zoo!' **SOLO.** **Allegro.** ♩=100.

six - pence for the 'Zoo!' He caused a most un-luck-y star To

six - pence for the 'Zoo!'

Allegro.

CHORUS.

(The Mer-chant with three daugh-ters;)

shine on Beau-ty's poor Pa - pa (The Mer-chant with three daugh-ters;) **SOLO.**

With

(The Mer-chant with three daugh-ters;)

(The Mer-chant with three daugh-ters;)

(The Mer-chant with three daugh-ters;)

W. 1625

hea-vy E-qui-noc-tial gales He tore his brigs' and schoon-ers' sails, And

cres:

scared the tars with spout-ing whales, That at the ves-sel frisk'd their tails, And

cres:

thump'd a-bout her quar-ters; Then all a-round the toss-ing ships, He

f

bid the sun with an e-clipse, And rais'd the an-gry wa-ters, And

ff rall:

rall: ff

Andantino.

thus the Mer-chant came to be Re-duc'd to gen-teel po-ver-ty Him-

p a tempo primo.

CHORUS.

And sin‿gle daugh‿ters three;..

_self and sin‿gle daugh‿ters three; And sin‿gle daugh‿ters three;.. **SOLO.** So

And sin‿gle daugh‿ters three;..

And sin‿gle daugh‿ters three;..

he left Town, and set‿tled down In coun‿tri‿fied ob‿scu‿ri‿

D. Moderato. ♩= 66.

CHORUS. _misterioso._

So he left Town, and set‿tled down In coun‿tri‿fied ob.
misterioso.

_ty._ So he left Town, and set‿tled down In coun‿tri‿fied ob.
misterioso.

So he left Town, and set‿tled down In coun‿tri‿fied ob.
misterioso.

So he left Town, and set‿tled down In coun‿tri‿fied ob.

scu _ri_ _ty._ So he left Town, and set _tled down_ In coun _tri_ _fied_ ou_

scu _ri_ _ty._ So he left Town, and set _tled down_ In coun_tri_ _fied_ ob_

scu _ri_ _ty._ So he left Town, and set _tled down_ In coun_tri_ _fied_ ob_

scu _ri_ _ty._ So he left Town, and set _tled down_ In coun_tri_ _fied_ ob_

scu _ri_ _ty,_

scu _ri_ _ty._

scu _ri_ _ty._

scu _ri_ _ty._

ob_scu_ _ri_ _ty,_ In coun_tri_ _

ob_scu_ _ri_ _ty,_ In coun_tri_ _

ob_scu_ _ri_ _ty,_ In coun_tri_ _

ob_scu_ _ri_ _ty._

CHORAL RECIT:—"ONE DAY CAME A MESSAGE."

One day came a message, hap-py but short, Say-ing, "Two of your ships have just come in-to port; You are wanted at once!" That was good news indeed, Ay, no doubt a-bout that, the three sis-ters agreed, Ay, no doubt a-bout that the three sis-ters agreed, Ay, no doubt a-bout that the three sis-ters agreed, And the Ay, no doubt a-bout that the three sis-ters agreed, Ay, no doubt a-bout that the three sis-ters agreed, elders at once thought it high time to frown At the life in a cottage, and get back to Town.— But the

SOP: 3

ALTI.
Had come

TEN: 3 3 3
Had come
The two ships that were reckon'd as lost by the wise, Had come

3 3 3
Merchant was really half-daz'd with surprise,
Had come

3 3 3
home, had come home, had come home. . . . . . . and in safe_ty!

A

3 3
home, had come home, had come home. . . . . . . and in safe_ty!

Solo.

3 3
home, had come home, had come home, ... and in safe_ty!
"Now,

3 3
home, had come home, had come home, ... and in safe_ty!

3 3 3 3
_dar_lings" said he, "I am off___ but I'll buy, I'll buy what you choose for all

ALTI
three," Then the elders replied, "Now you've mon_ey to spare, Bring us back all the fash_ions, we've
SOP:
"Bring us back all the fash_ions, we've nothing to wear!"
SOLO. SOP:
But the
nothing to wear, Bring us back all the fash_ions; we've no_thing to wear!"
young_est, Miss Beau_ty, most mo_dest_ly chose For her gift nothing more than a
rall:
col canto.
simple white Rose!
TENORI.
Her sis_ters at this laugh'd loud_ly, But let Pa_pa
BASSI.
Her sis_ters at this laugh'd loud_ly, But let Pa_pa
a tempo.
go To buy what they wish'd for and look af_ter his car_go.
go To buy what they wish'd for and look af_ter his car_go.

No. 4.

M.M. ♩=112.

Allegro Moderato.

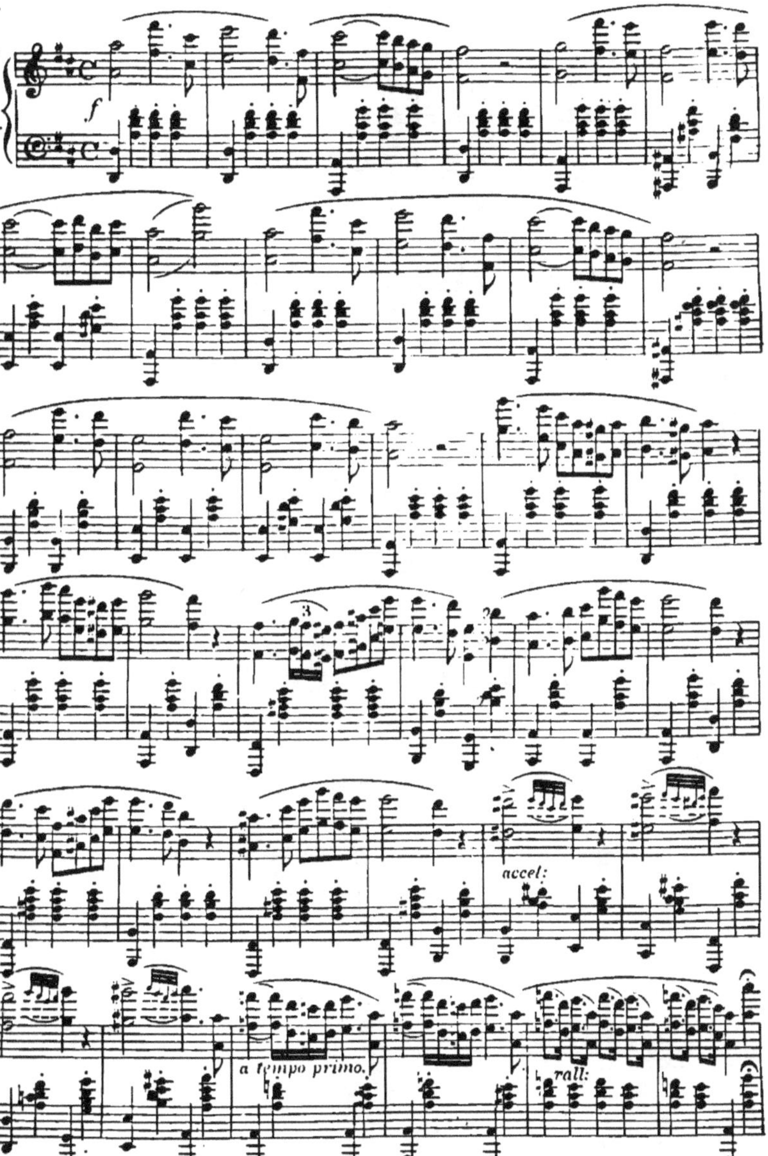

SOP:
ALTI.
TEN:
BASS.
f
Off went the old man, off.... went he, Mounted on his ca - mel,
Joy - ful - ly! Off went the old man, off.... went he,
Mount - ed on his ca - mel, Joy - ful - ly! Trotting o - ver hill and dale,

As it was his du _ ty, Singing "I must have a rose; Yes! the fair.est one that

As it was his du _ ty, Singing "I must have a rose; Yes! the fair.est one that

As it was his du _ ty, Singing "I must have a rose; Yes! the fair.est one that

As it was his du _ ty, Singing "I must have a rose; Yes! the fairest one that

grows, There is no such word as fail! There is no such word as fail!..

grows, There is no such word as fail! There is no such word as fail!..

grows, There is no such word as fail! There is no such word as fail!..

grows, There is no such word as fail! There is no such word as fail!..

accel:

I must get a pure white rose, I must get a pure white rose,

accel:

I must get a pure white rose, I must get a pure white rose,

accel:

I must get a pure white rose, I must get a pure white rose,

I must get a pure white rose, I must get a pure white rose,

accel:

a tempo primo.
A
ritard:
I . . . . shall find one I . . . . sup-pose, I shall find one I sup-pose,"
I shall find one I sup- -pose, I shall find one I sup-pose,"
I shall find one I sup- -pose, I shall find one I sup-pose,"
I shall find one I sup- -pose, I shall find one I sup-pose,"
a tempo
Off went the old man, off. . . . went he, Mount-ed on his
Off went the old man, off went he, Mount-ed on his
f
rall:
ca-mel, Joy- -ful- -ly! "I must get a pure white rose;
ca-mel, Joy-ful- - -ly!

And pop it un_der_neath the nose

"I shall find one I sup_pose.... And pop it un_der_neath the nose

And pop it un_der_neath the nose

"I shall find one I sup_pose.... And pop it un_der_neath the nose

Of my daugh_ter Beau_ty! Pop it un_der_neath the nose.

Of my daugh_ter Beau_ty! Pop it un_der_neath the nose.

Of my daugh_ter Beau_ty! Pop it un_der_neath the nose.

Of my daugh_ter Beau_ty! Pop it un_der_neath the nose.

Of my daugh_ter Beau_ty!"

Of my daugh_ter Beau_ty!"

Of my daugh_ter Beau_ty!"

Of my daugh_ter Beau_ty!"

Nº 5.

RECIT:—"BUT THE ENCHANTER."
(CONTRALTO.)

VOICE.

But the En_chanter, full of spite, Made the ca_mel kick and

PIANO.

bite; Rais'd a storm as well he could; Plant_ed

an.... en_chant_ed wood, Where there grew, in place of

trees, Gob_lin trunks, with gout_y knees; So the

Mer_chant, in his woes, Al_most had for_got the rose.

CHORUS.—"THOUGH THIS COULD TH'ENCHANTER DO."

Nº 6.

M.M. ♩ = 84.

Allegretto
Moderato.

p sempre leggiero.

1st SOP:

Though this could th'En-chant-er do, There was a good Fai-ry too; She, a friend both

2nd SOP:

Though this could th'En-chant-er do, There was a good Fai-ry too; She, a friend both

ALTI:

Though this could th'En-chant-er do, There was a good Fai-ry too; She, a friend both

true and tried, Always at the Merchant's side. There is dark, and there is light:

true and tried, Always at the Merchant's side. There is dark, and there is light:

true and tried, Always at the Merchant's side. There is dark, and there is light:

W. 1625.

32

All things have their op_po_site. Some are dirty, some are clean, Roast beef has its

All things have their op_po_site. Some are dir_ty, some are clean, Roast beef has its

All things have their op_po_site. Some are dir_ty, some are clean, Roast beef has its

fat and lean; Oceans have their ebb and flow; Sea_sons have their spring and snow.

fat and lean; Sea_sons have their spring and snow.

fat and lean;

Some are joy_ful, some are sad; There is al_ways good and bad: In this world of

Some are joy_ful, some are sad; There is al_ways good and bad: In this world of

Some are joy_ful, some are sad; In this world of

W. 1825.

fuss and bo_ther, There is one thing or an_o_ther. So, when things were
fuss and bo_ther, There is one thing or an_o_ther. So, when things were
fuss and bo_ther, So, when things were
at their worst, On the Mer_chant's vi_sion burst, Shi_ning in the
at their worst, On the Mer_chant's vi_sion burst, Shi_ning in the
at their worst, Shi_ning in the
A
summer air, Such a Fai_ry Cas_tle there!
summer air, Such a Fai_ry Cas_tle there!
summer air, Such a Fai_ry Cas_tle there! Mar_ble steps, and o_pen'd doors,
f

Pipes and cof - fee, cush - ion'd seat,
Silk - en cur - tains, po - lish'd floors, Pipes and cof - fee, cush - ion'd seat,
Silk - en cur - tains, po - lish'd floors, Pipes and cof - fee, cush - ion'd seat,
Slip - pers for his wea - ry feet; Sup - per rea - dy, to in - vite
Slip - pers for his wea - ry feet; Sup - per rea - dy, to in - vite
Slip - pers for his wea - ry feet; Sup - per rea - dy, to in - vite
B
His in - creas - ing ap - pe - tite; Fruits and flow'rs, and ev' - ry dish
His in - creas - ing ap - pe - tite;
His in - creas - ing ap - pe - tite;

J_der _ man could wish; But, what was the strang_est case,

d_der _ man could wish; But, what was the strang_est case,

M_der _ man could wish; But, what was the strang_est case,

al was in the place! Af_ter sup_per, Mer _ chant's head

al was in the place! Af_ter sup_per, Mer _ chant's head

al was in the place! Af_ter sup_per, Mer _ chant's head

a_fort_ _a_ _ble bed.___ Had his break_fast laid at eight,

a_fort_ _a_ _ble bed,___ Had his break_fast laid at eight,

a_fort_ _a_ _ble bed.___ Had his break_fast laid at eight,

Though there was no one to wait; Af-ter that he sat a-while;

Though there was no one to wait; Af-ter that he sat a-while;

Though there was no one to-wait; Af-ter that he sat a-while;

Then he thought to walk a mile. There were none to beg their par-don,

Then he thought to walk a mile. There were none to beg their par-don,

Then he thought to walk a mile. There were none to beg their par-don,

So he stroll'd a-bout the gar-den. Oh! such ter-ra-ces and bow'rs!

So he stroll'd a-bout the gar-den.

So he stroll'd a-bout the gar-den.

Oh! such foun_tains! Oh! such flow'rs! And oh, there! be_fore his nose,
Oh! such foun_tains! Oh! such flow'rs! And oh, there! be_fore his nose,
And oh, there! be_fore his nose,
Such, oh! such a charm_ing rose! And oh, there! be_fore his nose,
Such, oh! such a charm_ing rose! And oh, there! be_fore his nose,
Such, oh! such a charm_ing rose! And oh, there! be_fore his nose,
Such, oh! such a charm_ing rose!
Such, oh! such a charm_ing rose!
Such, oh! such a charm_ing rose!

RECIT:—"TO SEE WAS TO PICK."

No 7.

(CONTRALTO, TENOR & BASS.)

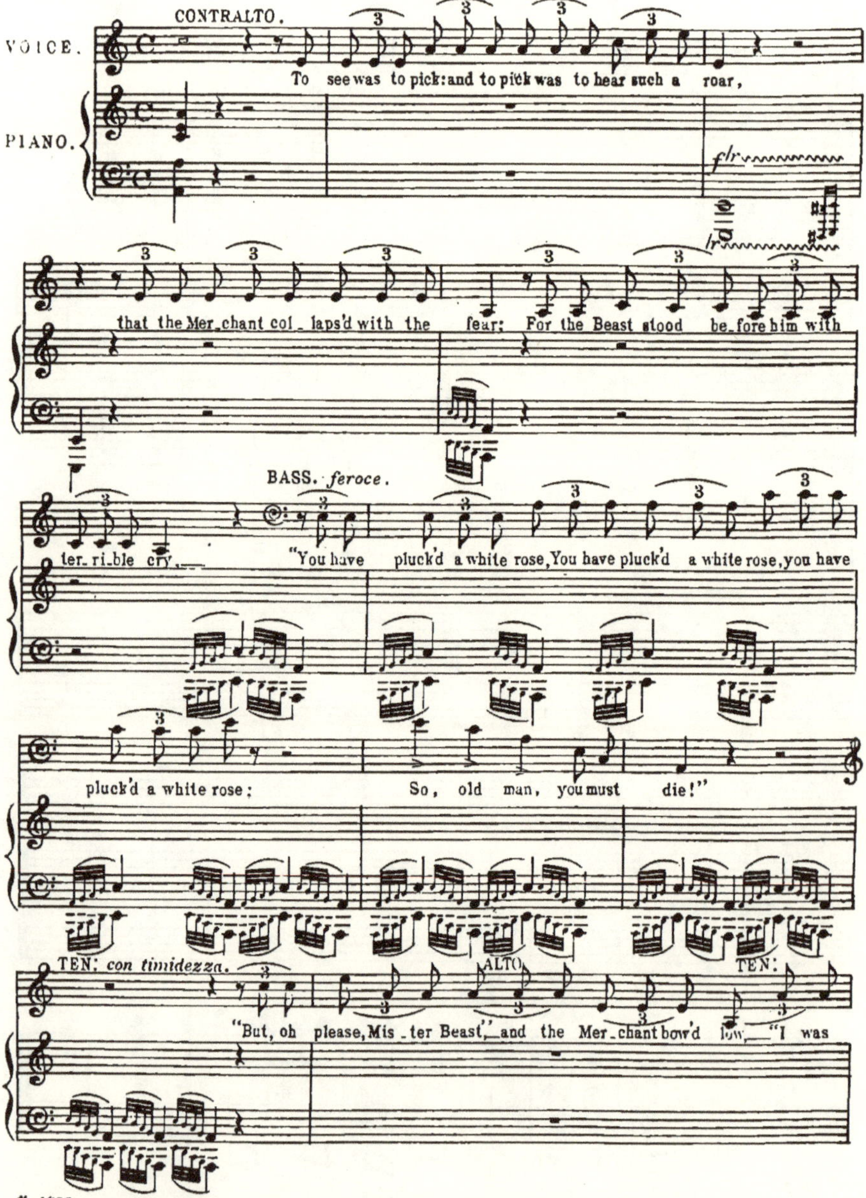

come in your stead, — I'm in want of a wife, — And
if the girl suits me, I'll grant your your life. — You a-
-gree to the bar-gain! Then go for your daugh-ter; For your
life's not worth two-pence un-til you have brought her."

con forza.

CHORUS.—"HOME CAME THE OLD MAN."

No. 8.

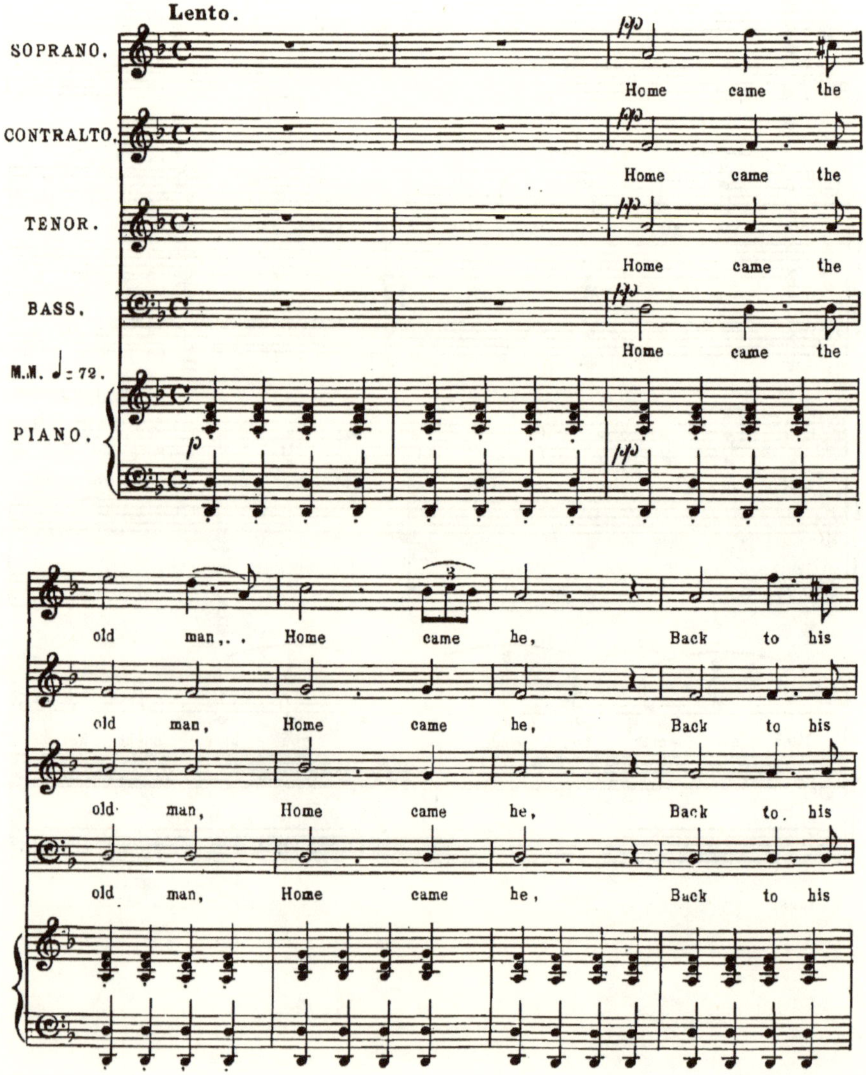

daugh - ters Mourn - ful - - ly! Home came the
daugh - ters Mourn - ful - ly! Home came the
daugh - ters Mourn - ful - ly! Home came the
daugh - ters Mourn - ful - ly! Home came the

old man, Home came he, Back to his
old man, Home came he, Back to his
old man, Home came he, Back to his
old man, Home came he, Back to his

daugh - ters, Mourn - ful - ly! Say - ing,
daugh - ters, Mourn - ful - ly! Say - ing,
daugh - ters, Mourn - ful - ly! Say - ing,
daugh - ters, Mourn - ful - ly! Say - ing,

ARIA.—(TENOR.) "OH! I AM VERY, VERY SAD."

Nº 9.

DUET (TENOR & SOPRANO.) & CHORUS.

Moderato.

VOICE.

M.M. ♩ = 80.

PIANO.

TENOR.

"Oh! I am ve_ry, ve_ry sad; Come a_long and kiss your

Dad, Come a_long and kiss your Dad, If you know your

LH.

Ped.   Ped.

du_ty One of you, my daugh_ters three, Soon a wretched bride must

LH.   LH.

Ped.   Ped.

W. 1625.

be. Or it is all up with me.___ Will you save me

Beau_ty! Or it is all up with me.___ So

rall:

will you save me Beau_ty!"

A

SOPRANO.

"Yes! my love has not de-

_creas'd, I will do my du_ty!" "But, my

TENOR.

SOPRANO.
dear, when he's a Beast!" "That don't mat_ter in the
LH.
Ped.
least! Yes! my love has not de_creas'd I will do my
CHORUS.
Prompt_ly an_swer'd Beau_ty.
Prompt_ly an_swer'd Beau_ty.
Prompt_ly an_swer'd Beau_ty.
Prompt_ly an_swer'd Beau_ty.
LH.
Ped.
TENOR.
SOPRANO.
du_ty!" "But, my dear, when he's a Beast!" "That don't mat_ter in the

rall:
least
TENOR.
"That don't matter in the least
That don't matter in the
"That don't matter in the least
That don't matter in the
CHORUS.
Prompt - ly an-swer'd
least!"
least!"
Beau-ty!
Beau-ty!
Beau-ty!

RECIT:_"TO THE BEAST'S PALACE."

Nº 10.

(CONTRALTO.)

Andantino.

VOICE.

To the Beast's Palace now we'll change the scene,

PIANO.

p   dolce.

With Beau-ty there as pam-pered as a queen.

p

Nº 11.

ARIA._"BY UNSEEN HANDS."

Andantino.   (SOPRANO.)

VOICE.

M. M. ♩ = 80.

PIANO.

p

By un_seen

hands she sees the co-vers luid; By un_seen power her

ev'- -ry wish o - bey'd; For her, fine silks by
un - seen hands are sewn; The fair - est fruits . . . by
un-seen gard'- ners grown. By un - - seen hands . . . . she
sees, she sees the co - vers laid; By un - - seen power . . her
ev'- ry wish o - bey'd. For her . . . . fine silks . . . . . by

un-seen hands are sewn; The fair - est fruits . . . . by
un-seen gard'-ners grown. And all . . . . a - round her
A
dolce.
speaks of wealth and gold For gems and jew - els
there are here un - told. And all . . . a - round . . . her
3
speaks of wealth, of wealth and gold For gems . . . . and . . jew - els
3

there are here un told. And Beau ty sits a glow with diamonds

rare And looks, as you may guess, sur.pass.ing fair And

Beau ty sits a glow with diamonds rare And looks, and

con forza.

looks, and looks as you may guess, as you may guess, sur pass ing

col canto.

fair.

RECIT: __ "AT CERTAIN HOURS."

Nº 12.

(CONTRALTO.)

VOICE.

At cer_tain hours, and on _ly by re _ quest, Walks in the

PIANO.

Beast,

The long ex_pect_ed guest. They sit at ta_ble; and be_fore they

part The Beast kneels down and of _ fers her his heart. . . .

W. 1625.

Nº 13.

(BASS.)

Allegro Vivace.

Recit:

"Say, do you love me!

Say, do you love me! do you love me!

a tempo.

Say, do you love me! Say, do you love me! Say, oh

say, oh say, do you love me! Oh say, do you love me! I'm rather rough in my ex_te_rior, Miss; I'm rather rough in my ex_te_rior, Miss; I'm rather

rough, I'm rather rough, I'm ra_ther rough, I'm ra_ther rough in my ex_te_rior,

Miss; but ster_ling stuff, but ster_ling stuff, but ster_ling stuff with_in my shaggy hide a

wife would find, but ster_ling stuff with _ in my shaggy hide a wife would find, a wife would

A

find. As I said be _ fore

I am ra-ther rough; To look up-on me you would think me

tough, As I said be-fore, I am ra-ther rough, To

look up-on me you would think... me tough. But no, my

heart is ve-ry ten-der, Miss, ve-ry ten-der, Miss, There-

-fore say "Yes," and give me one sweet kiss, give me one sweet kiss,

one sweet kiss. As I said be-fore, I am ra-ther rough; To look up-on me you would think me tough. As I said be-fore, I am ra-ther rough, To look up-on me you would think me... tough. But no, my heart is ve-ry ten-der, Miss, ve-ry ten-der, Miss, There-fore say

W. 1625.

"Yes," and give me one sweet kiss, give me one sweet kiss...

one sweet kiss. Say, do you love me! do you love me! Say, do you

love me! Say do you love me! Say, oh say, oh

say, do you love me! Oh say, do you love me! I'm rather

rough in my ex_te_rior, Miss; I'm rather rough in my ex_te_rior,

Miss; I'm ra_ther rough, I'm ra_ther rough, I'm ra_ther rough, I'm ra_ther rough in my ex_ter_ior, Miss; But ster_ling stuff, but ster_ling stuff, but ster_ling stuff with_in my shag_gy hide a wife would find, but ster_ling stuff with_in my shag_gy hide a wife would find a wife would find; but ster_ling stuff, but ster_ling

cres:

cres:

stuff, but ster_ling stuff with _ in my shag _ gy hide a wife would

find; but ster_ling stuff but ster_ling stuff but ster_ling

stuff with _ in my shag_gy hide a wife would find; but ster_ling

stuff with _ in my shag_gy hide a wife would find."

N.º 14.

RECIT: "OH, BEAST! SAID BEAUTY."

(SOPRANO, CONTRALTO & BASS.)

VOICE.

PIANO.

SOPRANO.

irresoluto.

"Oh, Beast!" said Beau_ty, "love is not so blind, ___ You're.

deciso.

ve_ry gen_tle for a Beast, 'tis true, ___ But say 'good_night', for I'm no match for

CONTRALTO.

you!" With one heart-rend_ing sigh The Beast has flown, And Beauty, as be_

accel: *ritard:*

_fore, is all a_lone. A_gain, at in_ter_vals, a_gain, a_gain, The Beast pleads

ur_gent_ly how great his pain; **Allegro vivace.**

ƒƒ Agitato.

W. 1625.

A *Recit:*

But Beau-ty, mov'd by kind-ness more and more. Re-

fu-ses with de-ci-sion, as be-fore,—— Al-though, the Beast sighs deep-ly at the

blow, When Beau-ty ut-ters her em-pha-tic "No!" Now in her

room a ma-gic mir-ror stood (The Beast was e-ver thought-ful for her good,)

And look-ing in it, Beau-ty, at her will, Could see her home, as if she lived there

Moderato.

B

still.

una corda.

Agitato.

One day, she looked and saw her fa_ther ill, His mouth ex_tend_ed to re_ceive a

pill; Her daugh_ter's heart with love was all a _ glow; "Oh Beast!" she

SOPRANO.

supplicando.

cried, *Dear Beast!* pray let me go!" With tears he an_swer'd

CONTRALTO.

BASS.

affettuoso

"I've no cause to doubt you, But come back soon, I can_not live without you!"

Nº 15.

(SOPRANO, CONTRALTO, TENOR, BASS) & CHORUS.

Moderato. CHORUS.

Soprano. Home came Beauty, Home came she; Saw her father well again, Well as he could be.

Contralto. Home came Beauty, Home came she; Saw her father well again, Well as he could be.

Tenor. Home came Beauty, Home came she; Saw her father well again, Well as he could be.

Bass. Home came Beauty, Home came she; Saw her father well again, Well as he could be.

M.M. ♩=80.

Piano.

TENOR SOLO.

"Now you'll stay with us," he cried, "Since you are not yet a bride,"

Ped.

SOPRANO.

"But I've promis'd" she re_plied "And I know my du_ty!"

Allegretto.
CONTRALTO.
"Oh, pooh, pooh! you sil_ly chit, Since you've had the chance to flit," Said her sis_ters,
p
"wait a bit!" "But I can't!" said Beau_ty.
SOP:
rall:
A
Moderato.
"For, in deed, I've had a
dream,
One that near_ly made me scream,
CHORUS.
misterioso.
She's had a dream,
One that near_ly made her scream,
LH.
Ped.

Telling her her du - ty,
Tell - ing her her du - ty.
Tell - ing her her du - ty,
Tell - ing her her du - ty.
Tell - ing her her du - ty,
Tell - ing her her du - ty.
Tell - ing her her du - ty,
Tell - ing her her du - ty.
LH.
LH.
Ped.
Ped.
I . . . saw that lov - ing Bear
Ly - ing flat as if he were
That lov - ing Bear,
Ly - ing flat,
That lov - ing Bear,
Ly - ing flat,
That lov - ing Bear,
Ly - ing flat,

Dead or faint-ing;—So, mon père, I'm off a-gain'' said

Dead or faint-ing, dead or faint-ing,

Dead or faint-ing, dead or faint-ing,

Dead or faint-ing, dead or faint-ing,

Dead or faint-ing, dead or faint-ing,

Beau-ty. "Dead or faint-ing.—so mon père, I'm

She's off a-gain! Dead or faint-ing, so she's

She's off a-gain! Dead or faint-ing, so she's

She's off a-gain! Dead or faint-ing, so she's

She's off a-gain! Dead or faint-ing, so she's

off a - gain!" said Beau-ty.

As

off, she's off a gain!

off, she's off a gain!

off, she's off a gain!

off, she's off a gain!

soon as she came to the Palace she found (For her dream was a true one) Poor Beast on the ground, He was

dy-ing, poor Beast! "Oh! I love you! I love you! I love you! I

SOPRANO.
con abbandono.

love.....you!" she cried "Oh! I love, I love.....

CONTRALTO.
BASSO.
affettuoso.
you!" And she flung her white arms round his shag-gy old hide. "You do love me" he whisper'd, "It
want-ed but this! As a Bear, let me hug you!"
CHORUS.
She gave him a kiss . . . . she gave him a kiss . . . .
She gave him a kiss . . . . she gave him a kiss . . . .
She gave him a kiss, she gave him a kiss, she gave him a kiss . . . .
She gave him a kiss, she gave him a kiss, she gave him a kiss . . . . . .

FINALE.

CHORUS.—"IN A SECOND OR LESS."

Nº 16.

M.M. ♩ = 132.

Allegro Moderato

SOPRANO.

In a second or less, deck'd with jewels and gold, A fair

CONTRALTO.

In a second or less, deck'd with jewels and gold, A fair

TENOR.

In a second or less, deck'd with jewels and gold, A fair

BASS.

In a second or less, deck'd with jewels and gold, A fair

Prince at her feet his love ardently told; And there was the Fai _ ry, who

Prince at her feet his love ardently . told; And there was the Fai _ ry, who

Prince at her feet his love ardently . told; And there was the Fai _ ry, who

Prince at her feet his love ardently told; And there was the Fai _ ry, who

W. 1625.

came with a smile, To un - do all the work of th'En - chant - er so vile;
came with a smile, To un - do all the work of th'En - chant - - er so vile;
came with a smile, To un - do all the work of th'En - chant - - er so vile;
came with a smile, To un - do all the work of th'En - chant - - er so vile;
There was the Fai ry who came with a smile,
There was the Fai - ry who came with a smile,
There was the Fai - ry who came with a smile,
There was the Fai - ry who came with a smile,
To un - do all the work of th'En - chant - er so vile;
To un - do all the work of th'En - chant - er so vile;
To un - do all the work of th'En - chant - er so vile;
To un - do all the work of th'En - chant - er so vile;

A
There was the Fai - ry who came with a smile,
To un - do all the work of th'En - chant - er so vile;
And her fa - ther was there, as if dropp'd from the skies;
As if dropp'd from the skies;
And her sis - ters were with him, in jea - lous, in jea - lous sur -
8va

Her fa_ther was there, as if dropp'd from the skies; And her
As if dropp'd from the
Her fa_ther was there, as if dropp'd from the skies; And her
As if dropp'd from the
B
ere with him', in jea_lous, in jea_lous sur - prise,
ere with him, in jea_lous, in jea_lous sur _ prise,
a - ther was there, as if dropp'd from the skies; And her
a - ther was there, as if dropp'd from the skies; And her
ther was there, as if dropp'd from the skies; And her
ther was there, as if dropp'd from the skies; And her

sis - ters were with him, in jea - lous sur-prise, Her sis - ters were there, Her
sis - ters were with him, in jea - lous sur-prise, Her sis - ters were there, Her
sis - ters were with him, in jea - lous sur-prise, Her sis - ters were there, Her
sis - ters were with him, in jea - lous sur-prise, Her
sis-ters were there, in jea-lous, in jea-lous sur - prise,
sis-ters were there, in jea-lous, in jea-lous sur - prise,
sis-ters were there, in jea-lous, in jea-lous sur - prise,
sis-ters were there, in jea-lous, in jea-lous sur - prise,
C
ff
And her father was there, as if
And her father was there, as if
And her father was there, as if
And her father was there, as if
ff

dropp'd from the skies; And her sis - ters were with him, in jea - lous sur-prise, And who
en - vied her luck 'till the Fai - ry so clever, Turn'd them both in to sta - tues to
frown on for e - ver.
accel - er - an - do.
Turn'd them both, turn'd them both, turn'd them both, turn'd them

both, Turn'd them in _ to sta _ tues to frown on for

e _ ver. Turn'd them both, turn'd them both, turn'd them both, turn'd them both, Turn'd them in _ to

sta _ tues to frown on for e _ ver. . . . .